Guide to
Indian
Herbs

Red Clover *Trifolium pratense*

E. Barrie Kavasch

By Raymond Stark

ISBN 0-88839-077-7
Copyright © 1981 Raymond Stark

Canadian Cataloging in Publication Data

Stark, Raymond
    Indian Herbs

    ISBN 0-88839-077-7

    1. Herbs - Identification.   2. Herbs -
Therapeutic use.   3. Botany, Medical - North
America.   4. Indians of North America -
Medicine.   I. Title
QK99.N67S83   581.6'34'097   C80-091255-1

Editor Margaret Campbell
Production Peter Burakoff
Layout/Design Vasilikki Makris and Diana Lytwyn
Typeset by Sandra Sawchuk and Anne Whatcott in Megaron
type on an AM Varityper Comp/Edit.
Line Drawings by Diana Lytwyn

Printed in Canada by Friesen Printers

Simultaneously published by

HANCOCK HOUSE PUBLISHERS LTD.
#10 Orwell St., North Vancouver, B.C. Canada V7J 3K1

HANCOCK HOUSE PUBLISHERS INC.
1431 Harrison Avenue, Blaine, Washington 98230, U.S.A.

Table of Contents

Introduction

Before European immigration to North America, and for some time afterwards, Indians maintained an extensive stock of herbal medicines which they gathered from the forests, plains and mountains of their locales.

In many Indian tribes and nations, the medicine man or medicine woman was much like a para-psychologist. Their function was to encourage the mind of the ailing person to turn toward a positive style of thinking, with (it was hoped) a corresponding start on the path to improvement.

In some Indian nations — such as the Ojibwa, Cherokee, and Creek — the work of the "medicine man" was complemented by that of the herbalist, the individual who treated a patient with roots, leaves, barks, and berries. The Ojibwa had four distinct classifications of medicine people. First, and highest ranking, were the holy men of the Midewiwin, the Medicine Society; next came the Wabenos, the Men of the Dawn, who practiced a kind of magic medicine, ensuring good fortune for warriors and hunters, providing incantations and charms. . . all the esoteric matters of magic. The herbs of forest and field were used in the rituals of the Wabenos, the success or failure of whose work depended upon a combination of natural medicines and human psychology.

Third in line were the Jessakid. These were the men of truth, of divination, the prophets and clairvoyants — the men who operated under the auguries of the God of the Thunder.

Last were the Doctors of Medicine, the Mashki-kike-winini, who knew the powers of the berries, leaves, roots, barks, resins, and flowers. These doctors of herbal medicine understood clearly that certain herbs exerted specific effects in the human body, and earnestly believed that the herbs functioned against some species of demonry held within the body.

This is somewhat analogous to the ancient Saxon belief that illnesses were caused by the evil elves of the air, land, and sea, and to be ill was to be "elf-shot." In modern medicine, we call these devils of the Indians and the elf-venom of the Saxon by such terms as bacteria, bacilli, microbes, viruses, and so on, but the basic theory appears to be much the same. None of them are fully understood, but all are treated by the best means available at the time.

Among the Ojibwa, women also served as herbal doctors, members of the Mashki-kike-winini, and some were members of the holy society of the Midewiwin.

Modern psychiatry is familiar with the idea that the psychology of the patient plays an important, if rather incomprehensible, part in healing. A present-day psychiatrist, for example, has his own special methods of affecting the psychology of the patient. . . the supine position, sedative medication, specific questions designed to relax, and so on. The Indian medicine man, with his rattles and bear claws and awesome paint, *expected* to impress the patient with his deliberately fearsome mien. The idea was that the Indian psychiatrist would look so fearsome and act in such a threatening way that the demons and evil spirits would be frightened away from the patient's body, *and the patient understood this.* This potent assistance from the medicine man must have bolstered the mental and emotional forces of the patient, and caused the physical ailment to respond positively.

More than 200 medicinal plants indigenous to the Americas have been official in the *United States Pharmacopoeia* since the first edition was published in 1820. In addition to these, perhaps another 300 herbs of the Indian world have been used by doctors, and a considerable number of these have been investigated by early pharmaceutical firms, and brought out under various names in the form of extracts or compounds or in synthetic forms.

Dandelion

E. Barrie Kavasch

Glossary

Amenorrhea: An abnormal absence or suppression of menstruation.

Amulets: Charms worn as remedy for or protection against evils or mischief, generally stones, metals, plants, words or characters arranged in a particular order.

Antispasmodic: A remedy or preventive for spasms.

Colic: Acute abdominal pain caused by various abnormal conditions of the bowels.

Debility: Weakness, feebleness, faintness or languor of the body.

Decoction: The process by which a substance is boiled in water to extract its essence.

Diaphoretic: A medical treatment promoting perspiration.

Diuretic: A drug promoting urinary discharge.

Dysentery: Any of various intestinal diseases characterized by inflammation, abdominal pain, toxemia and diarrhea.

Dyspepsia: Indigestion.

Emetic: A medicine or other substance causing vomiting.

Expectorant: A medicine causing the coughing up of phlegm or mucus.

Gonorrhea: A venereal disease.

Infusion: The process of pouring one substance into another.

Laxative: A medicine relaxing the muscles of the bowel, thus relieving constipation.

Lumbago: Backache, especially in the small of the back.
Neuralgia: Nerve pain.

Pleurisy: Inflammation of the pleural membrane surrounding the lungs, causing fever, pain, respiratory difficulty and a dry cough.

Poultice: A soft, hot, moist mass applied to sores or inflamed parts of the body.

Restorative: Medicine or treatment bringing back the patient to a former, normal or unimpaired condition.

Rhizome: A rootlike stem growing horizontally under or along the ground, sending out roots from its under surface and stems from its upper surface.

Stimulant: A drug that temporarily increases the activity of the vital process of an organ.

American Valerian
or Swamp Wood

Valeriana sylvatica

Europe has its medicinal Valerian, *Valeriana officinalis* — and so does North America with its American Valerian, *V. sylvatica*. This plant is prevalent in southern Canada and ranges southward to the Rocky Mountain region of New Mexico. It is primarily used as a sedative, and several tribes used the root for nervous problems, hysteria, and cardiac palpitations. The Blackfoot Indians used an infusion of American Valerian roots for stomach problems.

The Thompson Indians of British Columbia found the plant useful as an external treatment for wounds. The dried roots were powdered and sprinkled onto the wound as an antiseptic; the fresh roots were pounded and applied to the injured area; and the fresh leaves were chewed and placed on the wound.

Arborvitae
or Eastern White Cedar

Thuja occidentalis

This tree grows in northeastern Canada, and in the U.S. is found as far south as North Carolina and as far west as Minnesota.

The Canadian Ojibwa used a tea brewed from the leaves of the Arborvitae tree as a remedy for headache. Other Indian tribes of the United States and Canada used the leaves and bark of the Arborvitae to ease heart pains and headache, and to reduce swellings. Women of the Menominee tribe of Wisconsin drank a tea made from the inner bark of the Arborvitae to induce menstruation.

The leaves yield an oil which is valuable in the internal treatment of rheumatism and suppressed menstruation, and can induce abortion.

Many tribes made use of the inner bark of the tree as an emergency food in times of famine or momentary shortage.

American Valerian

Arborvitae

E. Barrie Kavasch

7

Arrowhead

Sagittaria latifolia

The Arrowhead plant or wapato was called swamp potato by the early settlers. It prefers to grow in shallow water and is found throughout North America except in the extreme north. Arrowhead tubers were a principal food for the Chinook and other tribes of the Pacific coast. The tubers were versatile food items; they could be eaten raw, despite the slightly bitter taste, or roasted like potatoes, and were highly nutritious.

The Arrowhead sets roots in the mud of shallow waters of lakes, ponds and similar bodies of water. Indian women usually collected the tubers, and this took a bit of doing. The women entered the water and, supporting themselves on a canoe, felt out the tubers with their toes. The loosened tubers rose to the surface of the water and were promptly gathered in. Attempts to pull the Arrowhead plant from the water simply break the plant off neatly and leave the tuber rooted in the mud, so toe-loosening the tubers was a highly efficient action.

The Chinook of Oregon were the main traders of the tubers of the Arrowhead to neighboring tribes who lacked supplies of the smooth bulbs. The leaves of the Arrowhead are cooling and astringent. They were used as poultices to stimulate blood flow.

E. Barrie Kavasch

Balsam Fir

Abies balsamea

This is a tree common to eastern North America.

The Maine Penobscot tribe applied the gum of the Balsam Fir as a healing covering for burns and sores, and several other tribes applied it to wounds and cuts. The Montana Chippewa and the Ottawa of the Great Lakes Region utilized a decoction of the inner bark of the Balsam Fir, mixed with tobacco leaves, as an inhalant to speed childbirth.

Balsam Poplar(Heart-leaved)
or Balm of Gilead
Populus candicans

This large tree grows throughout northeastern North America.

The Menominee Indians of Wisconsin made use of the resin-covered buds of the Poplar as an inhalant. These buds were boiled in fat to make an ointment, which was then used to stimulate the tissues of the respiratory tract. The Pillager Ojibwa used a similarly prepared ointment to relieve the congestion of colds, sinusitis, and bronchitis. The Potawatomis of lower Michigan concocted a salve by boiling the buds with mutton fat or bear tallow. This was applied to sores and eczema.

Several tribes prepared a tea from the leaves and bark which they used to relieve stomach disorders. A strong concoction of the same tea was believed efficacious if applied externally to cuts and burns.

The early colonists picked up the medicinal usage of the Poplars from the Indians, often adding whiskey to their preparations to ensure its potency.

Balsam Fir

Balm of Giliad

Black Cohosh

or Black Snakeroot

Cimicifuga racemosa

This leafy little plant grows in woods from Maine and Ontario to Wisconsin, and south as far as Georgia and Missouri.

The Nanticoke Indians of eastern Maryland and Delaware made a tonic tea of the root of Black Cohosh. The Winnebago and the tribes of the Dakota Nation took a decoction of Black Cohosh root to relieve rheumatism. It was also successful in treating pneumonia, asthma and croup.

However, the alternate name of "Squaw Root" explains the principle use of Black Cohosh by the majority of the tribes of eastern North America. It was particularly effective in treating all uterine complaints, particularly amenorrhea. The Delaware of Ontario and the northeastern United States used a root decoction for vaginal irritation. The same root decoction was found to be helpful for gonorrhea.

Between 1820 and 1936, Black Cohosh was listed in the *United States Pharmacopoeia*. During that period, the root and rhizome were recommended for the promotion of menstruation and as a sedative to relieve rheumatism.

E. Barrie Kavasch

E. Barrie Kavasch

Black Nightshade

POISONOUS

Solanum nigrum

Black Nightshade, a low leafy plant with small flowers that yield green berries, ripening to black, was introduced from Europe and was gathered on the Columbia River at Baker's Bay as early as 1825. The plant is now widely distributed, growing as far north as the Northwest Territories and as far south as Florida and Texas. Every part of the plant contains solanine, a poisonous alkaloid.

The Houma of Mississippi and Louisiana, the Comanche of Texas, and the Virginia Rappahannock all had several medicinal uses for Black Nightshade. They learned to destroy its poisonous properties by long slow cooking. The Rappahannock tribe treated insomnia by steeping the ripe berries in the water to make a beverage for the sufferer. All three tribes found the plant beneficial for tuberculosis and the expulsion of worms.

E. Barrie Kavasch

Burdock
or Cocklebur
Arctium lappa

Cocklebur is most commonly found in the area bounded by New Brunswick, Ontario and New York, and of all the docks was the one most frequently used for Indian ills. Only year-old roots were used and these were dug in the early spring or late fall.

The Flambeau Ojibwa prepared a tonic from the root of the common Cocklebur, and also used it to relieve stomach pains. The Meskwaki of Minnesota and Wisconsin administered the root as part of a compound medicine when their women were in labor. The Dakota and Cheyenne made ritual use of the Cocklebur, while the Otoe boiled the root in water and drank the resulting liquid as a remedy for pleurisy.

The Potawatomi drank a tea made from Cocklebur root as a tonic and blood-purifier. The early colonists followed suit, using the root in the preparation of a blood purifying drink, and of a wash to treat skin diseases.

E. Barrie Kavasch

Butternut

Juglans cinerea

Several Indian tribes of the north-central United States made medicinal use of various parts of the Butternut tree.

The Menominee, Meskwaki, and Potawatomi regarded the syrup and bark as valuable medicines in digestive problems. Some Indian tribes applied the crushed bark of this tree to areas of toothache, headache, and rheumatism. A strong decoction of the bark was used to treat fresh wounds.

Early doctors of the frontier found the properties of the Butternut tree as beneficial as did the Indians.

E. Barrie Kavasch

E. Barrie Kavasch

Canada Elder

TOXIC

Sambucus canadensis

This shrub is found in the lowlands from Nova Scotia to Florida, and westward to Manitoba, Kansas, and Texas. However, there are many related species and several of them, notably *S. pubens* and *S. coerules,* were extensively used in Indian medicine. Each species varied in its edibility — the one that produced blue berries, for instance, made excellent eating, but the species that had red berries was avoided by the Indians. Great care must be taken, therefore, in identifying this particular plant.

The Choctaw of Mississippi and Louisiana pounded Elder leaves, mixed them with salt, and used this preparation to relieve headaches. The neighboring Chickasaw made similar use of Canada Elder leaves. The leaves, bark and roots are highly toxic to poisonous. Only blossoms and ripe berries were used as food.

The Menominee drank a tea of the flowers to reduce fevers, while the Houma boiled the bark and used the liquid as a wash for inflammations. Other Indian tribes had different medical uses for the Canada Elder. The colonists also recognized the medicinal virtues of the Canada Elder.

E. Barrie Kavasch

E. Barrie Kavasch

Canadian Fleabane

Erigeron canadense

Canadian Fleabane is a common plant throughout North America. It has also become naturalized in Europe, where it grows in profusion as a weed.

The Canadian Cree Indians boiled the Canadian Fleabane plant in water and drank the tea as a remedy for digestive problems. The Catawba, Ojibwa, Meskwaki, and Houma tribes were known to make use of Canadian Fleabane for such irregularities as hemorrhage, digestive problems, and menstrual disorders. White doctors recorded many other Indian uses for the plant, notably as a palliative for rheumatism, hemorrhoids and gonorrhea.

The oil from the Canadian Fleabane plant, known as oil of Erigeron, was listed as a uterine stimulant in the *United States Pharmacopoeia* from 1863 to 1916.

E. Barrie Kavasch

Canadian Hemp

POISONOUS

Apocynum cannabinum

This tall plant with its delicate pink flower bells is abundant in the fields and thickets of Canada and the Northern United States. Many Indian tribes throughout this area found the root of the Canadian Hemp plant useful in the treatment of various diseases. It has been found to contain apocynin, tannin, and other useful medical components.

The Flambeau Ojibwa steeped the root of Canadian Hemp and administered the resulting liquid to women to keep the kidneys functioning normally during pregnancies. The Pillager Ojibwa considered the root sacred and employed it in medicine-lodge rituals. Both branches of the Canadian Ojibwa used the root of Canadian Hemp to relieve headache and throat irritation.

Both the forest and prairie Potawatomi used the plant — the men of the forest as a diuretic, the men of the prairie as a worm medicine — for their horses. The dried root has been used by non-Indians as a diuretic, as an emetic, as an expectorant, and to promote perspiration.

Cascara

Rhamnus purshiana

Cascara, a plant widely used in medicine, was borrowed from the Indians of the Pacific Coast.

A number of tribes made use of the bark of the Cascara tree as a laxative. Narrow strips of bark were peeled from the tree, dried, and aged for a year. The Thompson Indians of British Columbia boiled a small quantity of the bark in water to prepare a liquid laxative medicine.

Early Spanish priests learned of its superlative medicinal qualities from the Yokia Indians of Mendocino County, California and named it *Cascara sagrada,* the sacred bark.

In 1877, Dr. J.H. Bundy of Colusa, California, brought the bark to the attention of the medical profession. That same year, Parke, Davis & Company marketed a Cascara laxative preparation.

Cascara was adopted into the *United States Pharmacopoeia* in 1890, where it has remained ever since.

J.E. Underhill

Cattail

Typha latifolia

The Cattail is found throughout North America. This plant of the ponds, lakes, and marshes was much esteemed by the Indians as a cure for diarrhea. They ate the flowering heads for this purpose.

It was also a staple food. Several tribes cut the young shoots in the spring, peeled off the leaves and ate the inner portion as a raw vegetable. The Paiute tribe of Nevada and California ate the young flower stalks either fresh or boiled. The flowers were consumed singly, or in soups, stews, breads, and puddings. The sap was relished as "candy."

The young rootstocks were eaten after the peel was removed. The rootstocks were also made into flour through a process of drying and pulverizing, then removing the fibers. The seeds also served the Indians as food.

The down of the Cattail was employed to stuff pillows and mattresses, and was used as tinder, so that virtually nothing of the Cattail plant went to waste.

E. Barrie Kavasch

Common Camass

Camassia quamash

The Common Camass bears blue flowers. It should never be confused with the poisonous Death Camass, *C.zygademus spp.,* which has white to cream-colored flowers. The bulbs of the Common Camass were of prime importance to north-western Indian tribes—so much so that intertribal wars were fought for the privilege of gathering the edible tubers. The bulbs were baked for eating, or dried for future use. Fresh, raw Camass bulbs are crisp but almost tasteless. They were also mashed and made into a poultice for various ailments.

In a sense, the Camass plant helped to start the Nez Perce war with the white man. For countless springs the Nez Perce tribe had gathered the Camass from their traditional fields in the south and conducted ritual celebrations of its bounty. But when Chief Joseph of the Idaho Nez Perce led his People from their Clearwater River Reservation in Idaho to the Camass grounds, he provoked a confrontation with the Army.

J.E. Underhill

Cow·Parsnip

Heracleum lanatum

This vigorous, woolly plant grows in moist ground throughout Canada and Alaska, and is found as far south as California and North Carolina.

The Menominee, Meskwaki, and Ojibwa pounded the acrid roots of Cow-Parsnip and applied them as poultices on wounds and sores. When the problem was a headache or cramps, a root-poultice was applied to the afflicted body area. The roots were also a part of certain Indian religious rituals. Poultices were also recommended for sore throats, and ground root was sometimes blown into the throat as a treatment for diptheria. Pieces of the raw root were stuffed into cavities as a treatment for toothache, and the juice was used in ear infections.

The Cow-Parsnip also served the Indians as an article of food. The stems and young leaf-stalks were boiled in two changes of water to become an acceptable vegetable; tender stalks and stems were sometimes peeled and eaten raw, and the large root was boiled for food. The young leaves were eaten raw as a salad item.

The Cow-Parsnip is a good emergency food.

J.E. Underhill

Culver's Root

Veronicastrum virginicum

The Seneca of Ontario and the Allegheny Mountains in the United States made a tea of the root of Culver's Root and drank it for its laxative effect. The Meskwaki and Menominee employed Culver's Root for similar reasons. The Menominee also used the plant for ritual purification. The Meskwaki treated constipation with the root, used it to counter chills, and administered it as a tea to women in labor, or to those who were affected by general debility.

The pioneers learned the uses of Culver's Root from the Indians, their physicians finding it helpful in treating pleurisy, and as an emetic and cathartic.

Dandelion

Taraxacum officinale

Although this weed was introduced from Europe, it has become one of North America's most common herbs.

Tribes of the Iroquois Confederation of New York State made use of the common Dandelion as a food plant with hidden medicinal values. The Iroquois liked the leaves cooked with fat meat. Thus, the Indians had themselves a good-tasting green, and a good source of Vitamins A and C as well.

Other tribes employed the plant directly for its medicinal properties. A root tea was considered efficacious for yellow jaundice and liver and kidney complaints. The Pillager Ojibwa drank it for heartburn. The Mohicans drank a similar tea for its tonic qualities, but used the leaves instead of the root.

All over the world, the fresh young spring leaves of the Dandelion plant have been used for salad, the flowers for wine. The dried, roasted and ground root is still being sold for use as coffee.

Culver's Root

E. Barrie Kavasch

Dandelion

J.E. Underhill

Devil's Club

Echinopanax horridum

British Columbian Indians discovered that the root-bark of Devil's Club could counteract the weakening effects of diabetes. When this remedy was subjected to clinical testing, it was found that an extract of Devil's Club lowered the blood-sugar level in rabbits.

Among the Thompson Indians of British Columbia, Devil's Club was a standard tonic and blood purifier. The Bella Bella and other tribes of the Pacific Coast boiled the bark in water and drank the liquid as a cleansing emetic and as a cure for syphillis and the common cold. The bark was rubbed onto the body to remove scent and to ensure good endurance before a long hunt.

Medicine men of the coast tribes wore amulets made of Devil's Club when they invoked the assistance of the gods. Among the fishermen of the tribes, four pieces of Devil's Club bark placed in the canoe ensured a good catch.

Dogwoods

Cornus florida and other species

Because the various species of this tall shrub contain cornine, the bark was a favorite fever remedy of several Indian tribes.

The Houma used the bark of the southern species of Dogwood, *Cornus florida,* as their remedy for fevers. Among the Alabama, Potawatomi, Meskwaki, and Menominee tribes, the liquid from an infusion of the bark was sometimes held in the mouth to relieve aching teeth or facial neuralgia. The liquid was also employed as a wash for leg pains.

White settlers learned the medicinal properties of Dogwood bark from the Indians, using it mainly for fevers and colic.

Devil's Club

Dwarf Dogwood

J.E. Underhill

J.E. Underhill

False Solomon's Seal

Smilacina racemosa

One of the lily family, this plant has a cluster of small white flowers, red berries, and an extensive root system. The Nevada Shoshoni drank a leaf tea of False Solomon's Seal as a contraceptive. Conception was believed inhibited if sexual partners drank a half-cupful of the leaf tea daily for at least a week. A root tea was drunk by Shoshoni women as a remedy for menstrual disorders. Some tribes maintained it would also cure venereal disease.

The Blackfoot Indians used the dried and powdered root of False Solomon's Seal as an external treatment for wounds, sores and boils.

The Ojibwa and other tribes of Wisconsin, Oregon, and British Columbia ate the slightly bitter, pale red berries and the young shoots, and prepared the starchy rootstocks as a boiled vegetable.

Wm. Merilees

J.E. Underhill

23

Ginseng

Panax quinquefolium

There are two species of Ginseng, *Panax trifolium* **and** *Panax quinquefolium* The latter species occurs in Canada and the United States. Although it is fairly difficult in modern times to locate the plant in the wild, it is cultivated in shady locations in both countries.

The Indians had their uses for Ginseng root, although they did not share the Oriental regard for it as a panacea. Penabscot women steeped a piece of Ginseng root in water and periodically drank the resulting liquid as a means of increasing fertility. The Alabama Creek Indians drank a tea made from the roots for coughs, fevers, colds, hoarseness, and shortness of breath. They also rubbed the juice of the root on wounds and sores to aid healing. Several other tribes utilized the root of Ginseng. It was the main ingredient in a love potion made by the Meskwaki, and was gathered by both the Ojibwa and Meskwaki for sale to white traders, who dealt in export.

E. Barrie Kavasch

Gold Thread

Coptis trifolia

Gold Thread grows in damp, mossy woods and bogs across Canada and south as far as Maryland and Minnesota.

The Montagnais Indians of Newfoundland and Nova Scotia gave the name of Yellow Plant to the Gold Thread. They boiled it to make a tea which they used as a wash for sore eyes, lips, and the inside of the mouth.

The Pillager Ojibwa, Menominee, Mohican, and Penobscot tribes all made use of the plant, in one form or another, as a remedy for sore throat, mouth canker, and sore gums. The Potawatomi and New England doctors of colonial times had almost identical uses for Gold Thread; both used the plant as a tonic in dyspepsia and a remedy for general debility.

Gold Thread was listed in the *United States National Formulary* **between 1916 -1936.**

E. Barrie Kavasch

Highbush Cranberry

Viburnum opulus

This shrub is found in woods from New Brunswick to North Carolina.

The Malecite Indians of New Brunswick and northeastern Maine made a tea of Highbush Cranberry root and drank the liquid to cure mumps. This was also a practice of the Maine Penobscot.

Several tribes used the bark as a diuretic. The Pillager Ojibwa made a brew of the inner bark and drank it to correct stomach cramps. The Meskwaki boiled the bark in water and drank the liquid for cramps and general body pains.

The dried bark of the Highbush Cranberry was accepted by the medical profession for use as a sedative and antispasmodic. It was listed in the *United States Pharmacopoeia* between 1894-1916, and in the *National Formulary* between 1916-1960.

J.E. Underhill

E. Barrie Kavasch

26

Indian Turnip

TOXIC

Arisaema triphyllum

The Indian Turnip grows in moist woods and thickets in the area bounded by Nova Scotia, Florida, Kansas and Ontario.

The dried root of the Indian Turnip served the Shawnee and Osage as a remedy for coughs and intermittent fevers. The Pawnee, on the other hand, powdered it and sprinkled it on the temples and the top of the head as a remedy for headache. The root was used by the Iroquois as both food and medicine.

Other Indian tribes who found the dried root of the Indian Turnip beneficial for various ailments were the Menominee, Meskwaki, Ojibwa, and Penobscot. White physicians found the dried root useful in treating coughs, asthma, rheumatism, and colic.

Because of its extreme acridity, the root is never used in the fresh state. It is made edible by boiling.

E. Barrie Kavasch

E. Barrie Kavasch

E. Barrie Kavasch

Juniper

Juniperus communis

This shrub grows on dry hills in most areas of North America, and its blue berry has long been coveted as a flavoring.

The Canadian Cree dried Juniper leaves, pulverized them, and sprinkled the powder on stubborn sores. A tea made from the root was prescribed for kidney problems. The Kwakiutl of northwestern British Columbia boiled parts of the Juniper until the gum was released, then took the gum internally as a blood purifier and to relieve shortness of breath. The twigs were often toasted and formed into a hot pack for rheumatism or sore throats, and a solution made by boiling the twigs was used to hasten the eruption of measles and smallpox. The Zuni of New Mexico made a tea of Juniper leaves for use as a muscular relaxant following childbirth.

Juniper also served the Indians as an emergency food. The berries are tart and edible, and the inner bark can be eaten. Some Indians roasted the berries, ground them, and brewed them into a kind of coffee.

J.E. Underhill

Magnolia

Magnolia glauca (var.)

This flowering tree, a native of eastern North America, prefers to grow in swampy ground.

The Mississippi Choctaw and the Louisiana Houma were familiar with the medicinal virtues of the Magnolia. The tribes made the bark into a tea as a remedy for chills and cramps. The Louisiana Choctaw turned to the bark of a closely-related species of *Magnolia glauca* as a treatment for fevers and rheumatism.

Colonial doctors described Magnolia bark as a tonic, a stimulant, and perspiration-producing, and prescribed it mainly for intermittent fevers and inflammatory rheumatism.

Mayapple

POISONOUS

Podophyllum peltatum

This plant is native to eastern North America. It is similar to the European Mandrake, *Mandragora officinarum,* and is sometimes called American Mandrake. It can be poisonous if taken carelessly.

The Penobscot Indians of the northeastern United States applied the crushed root of the mayapple to warts. But most Indian tribes made use of the root internally as a purgative. Some Indians, understanding the potency of the plant, used the root to commit suicide, and there were occasional accidental poisonings among the tribes.

Early settlers adopted mayapple from the Indians and absorbed it into their own folk medicine. In modern times, this plant is usually employed as medicine but only under the supervision of a qualified herbal physician.

Mayapple Blossom

Mayapple unfolding

E. Barrie Kavasch

E. Barrie Kavasch

Mullen

Verbascum thapsus

This weed was naturalized from Europe and spread from Nova Scotia to Florida and west as far as Minnesota. There are several species and they have provided a variety of remedies.

Members of a number of North American Indian tribes smoked the dried leaves of Mullen to relieve asthma. The Menominee smoked the powdered dried root as a remedy for respiratory complaints which probably included what are now diagnosed as colds, influenza, asthma, and bronchitis.

The Catawba made a sweetened syrup from the boiled root, administering it to children who were afflicted with coughs. The leaves were mashed and used as a poultice for headaches, pains, swellings, wounds, bruises, and sprains. The chemicals found in Mullen soothe inflamed tissues and, when taken internally, calm nervous excitement and induce sleep.

Mullen was also used by white doctors, principally as a cough remedy.

Pearly Everlasting

Anaphalis margaritacea

This modest plant is found throughout southern Canada and the northern United States, ranging southward to West Virginia, and westward to northern California.

Many Indian tribes dried this herb and used it as smoking tobacco. It was believed to relieve respiratory distress. The Flambeau Ojibwa apparently also found the plant beneficial in cases of paralysis. The blossoms were crushed and burned, and the paralysis victim inhaled the smoke.

In colonial medicine, the plant was sometimes employed in the form of tea as a remedy for intestinal spasms and lung problems. Externally the tea was also applied to bruises. Pearly Everlasting has been used to treat coughs, colds, and fevers.

Mullen   Pearly Everlasting

B.C. Parks   J.E. Underhill

Pennyroyal

Hedeoma pulegioides

This aromatic herb grows in dry fields, from Cape Breton Island to Ontario, Minnesota, Nebraska, and south to Florida.

Pennyroyal tea was a favorite medicine. A mild stimulant, it was used particularly to reduce fevers. The Onondaga of the Iroquois Confederation drank the tea as a remedy for headaches. The Mohicans made use of a similar tea as a stomach tonic, and many Indian women drank it to ease the discomforts of menstruation. The Catawba boiled the plant in water and drank the liquid as a means of relieving the miseries of colds.

The Mescalero and Lipan Apache of the American southwest used a related species of Pennyroyal, *Hedeoma reverchoni*, to quell violent headaches. The Apache method was to rub the twigs of the plant and inhale the fragrance.

European Pennyroyal or True Pennyroyal, *Mentha pulegium*, is used for the same medicinal purposes as the North American Pennyroyal.

Pipsissewa

Chimaphila umbellata

This perennial herb flourishes in dry woods throughout North America.

The Thompson Indians of British Columbia pulverized the whole, fresh Pipsissewa plant and applied the moist mass to leg and foot swellings. The Penobscot and Mohican tribes infused Pipsissewa in warm water and applied the liquid to draw out blisters. The Canadian Montagnais, the mountain people, boiled the plant and used the liquid intentionally to promote perspiration. The Monominee used the plant as a remedy in women's disorders. The Catawaba steeped the plant in water and applied the liquid to relieve backache.

Pipsissewa has a respected place in folk medicine, where it is used mostly to induce perspiration and to ease rheumatism and kidney problems.

Pennyroyal

Pipsissewa

E. Barrie Kavasch

J.E. Underhill

Poke or Pokeweed

TOXIC

Phytolacca americana

This is a strong-smelling, succulent herb that grows freely in eastern North America.

Members of the Virginia Pamunkey tribe drank an infusion of Poke berries as a remedy for rheumatism. Appalachian folk doctors followed the Pamunkey medical practice, prescribing Poke-berry wine for rheumatism.

The Iroquois and other tribes held the Poke plant in esteem. The roots and berries were used variously to produce a blood purifier, a remedy for rheumatism, and an emetic to produce vomiting.

The leaves and young shoots of the Poke plant can be eaten as spring greens. However, because the plant — the root in particular — is toxic, it is wise to boil the Poke in two changes of water, and use it with caution.

Root and berries

E. Barrie Kavasch

E. Barrie Kavasch

Pulsatilla

or Pasque Flower

Anemone patens (var.)

This perennial herb prefers dry prairie soil.

The Omaha used the Pulsatilla as an external treatment for rheumatism and neuralgia. The fresh Pulsatilla leaves were crushed and placed on the ailing part of the body as a counter-irritant.

The Canadian Thompson Indians used Pulsatilla blossoms to stop nosebleed. The blossoms were held to the nose until bleeding stopped, or sometimes the leaves were inserted into the nostrils to achieve the same effect.

The Indian doctors of several tribes used the Pulsatilla and other species of *Anemone* in an external application to wounds, burns, boils and sore eyes. The plant also was favored by colonial physicians for treating sterility, and to induce menstruation.

Purple Boneset

or Joe-Pye Weed

Eupatorium purpureum

This perennial, also called Tall Boneset, grows in moist soil from New Brunswick to Manitoba, Florida and Texas. This plant came to be called Joe -Pye weed because Joe Pye, a New England Indian physician, reportedly managed to cure typhus with it by inducing copious perspiration.

Many tribes had various uses for the plant. The Delawares prepared a cold infusion of Purple Boneset as a wash for complexion improvement. This wash was applied every day over a considerable period of time. The Iroquois and the Cherokee of Georgia, North Carolina and Tennessee found the Purple Boneset beneficial as a diuretic. The Wisconsin Potawatomi made use of the fresh leaves as a poultice for burns and scalds.

During the colonial period, the root and rhizome of the Purple Boneset were used as astringents and diuretics.

Pulsatilla

Al & Jude Grass

Purple Boneset

E. Barrie Kavasch

Red Clover

Trifolium pratense

Red Clover — now a common plant in North America — is a well-known plant in the folk medicine of Europe. It has been used chiefly as a tonic, and for liver and gallbladder problems.

The Indians of Canada and the United States were enthusiastically acquainted with Red Clover, but valued it chiefly for its nutritional capabilities. Medicine seldom entered the picture.

The Digger Indians of northern California cooked Red Clover in a stone oven, placing a number of moistened layers of the plant inside, one upon the other. The Apache of the southwest made up a "mess of greens," boiling Red Clover with Dandelion, Pigweed, and various local grasses. The California Pomos staged special Clover feasts and celebrations when the plant appeared in the early spring.

Rose

Rosa species

Just about all the Indian tribes of North America took advantage of the Wild Rose species that flowered in their vicinities. From the mountain Apache of the southwestern United States to the Indians of British Columbia, to Ontario to Newfoundland and New England, the Rose predominated as a medicine — and the Rose hips contributed their sizable stores of Vitamin C.

The tribes of the Rocky Mountains boiled the roots of the Rose as a remedy for colds and fevers. The liquid also served as a treatment for diarrhea, influenza, liver and stomach disorders. A tea of the petals was reputed to function as a heart tonic. A tea of Rose hips was prescribed as a restorative, particularly in cases of tuberculosis, while decocted Roses were said to combat gonorrhea.

Red Clover

Smooth Rose

Rose hips

E. Barrie Kavasch   E. Barrie Kavasch

Sassafras

Sassafras albidum

This rough-barked tree grows in dry, sandy soil and is found from Massachusetts to Ontario, Michigan, Florida and Texas.

The Delawares made a tea from the inner bark and small dried roots of the Sassafras tree. This was used as a tonic and blood purifier. Most tribes of eastern North America, including the Virginia Rappahannock Indians, drank a tea of Sassafras roots to reduce fever, and to induce the initial appearance of the red rash of measles.

Sassafras root, or the stronger root-bark, is still in use all over North America, mostly as a tonic and a home method of lowering the blood pressure. Sassafras tea is often employed as a remedy against the common cold.

Safrole, the active ingredient of Sassafras, is used as a dental antiseptic, and as an ingredient in toothpastes, root beer, and chewing gums. Safrole, in large quantities, has also been found to function as a hallucinogenic drug. It has been listed as carcinogenic, after extensive research on all parts of the plant.

J. Pawloski

Skullcap

or Mad-Dog Weed

Scutellaria lateriflora

This bitter herb is widely distributed in the swamps of North America.

Cherokee women employed an infusion of Skullcap and three other plants to promote menstruation. Skullcap was also used in purification ceremonies, and to treat breast pains and diarrhea. The Flambeau Ojibwa made use of the Marsh Skullcap, *Scutellaria galericulata,* as a cardiac tonic. The Meskwaki found the Small Skullcap, *Scutellaria parvula,* useful in dysentery.

White doctors picked up the use of Skullcap for rabies, as a sedative and antispasmodic. The dried herb was listed in the *United States Pharmacopoeia* between 1863-1916 and in the *National Formulary* between 1916-1947.

Senega

TOXIC

Polygala senega

Senega, or Seneca Snakeroot, is found in rocky woods in most of the mountainous areas of North America.

Seneca Snakeroot owes its medicinal efficacy to the saponins contained in the dried root. In anything but small doses, the saponins are poisonous. The plant was in wide use among the Indians as a snakebite remedy, but at least two tribes — the Ottawa and the Chippewa — used it to produce abortion.

As the name implies, Seneca Snakeroot was popularized as a snakebite medicine by the Seneca of the Iroquois Confederation. However, the plant was adopted by the medical profession as a treatment for pleurisy, pneumonia, asthma, and other respiratory ailments.

Skullcap

Al & Jude Grass

Skunk Cabbage

Use with Caution

Symplocarpus foetidus

This rank-smelling plant is a denizen of the swamps of eastern North America, ranging westward to Manitoba and Iowa. It has a bright yellow, partially rolled flower that appears before the leaves start their growth.

The plant is mildly narcotic, antispasmodic, diuretic, emetic, and expectorant. However, an overdose of the root of Skunk Cabbage can be poisonous.

Many Indian tribes made use of the Skunk Cabbage for its tendency to quiet muscle spasms. The Delawares steeped the leaves in whiskey to make a remedy for tuberculosis. The root of Skunk Cabbage has been used to treat bronchitis, mucous congestion, whooping cough, asthma, and hay fever. Some Indians boiled the root-hairs of Skunk Cabbage and used the liquid to curb external bleeding. Externally, the mashed root was used on boils, swellings, and blood poisoning.

E. Barrie Kavasch

Slippery Elm

Ulmus fulva

This tree grows in woods, on hills and beside streams. Its habitat extends to North Dakota, Florida and Texas.

The Pillager Ojibwa made a tea from the inner bark of the Slippery Elm tree and used it to treat sore throats. The Catawba used Slippery Elm bark in infusion to treat tuberculosis, and also prepared a salve for external application in instances of painful rheumatism. The fresh bark was peeled and mixed with lard. The Creek employed the bark as a remedy for toothache. The Delawares soaked strips of the bark in hot water for a beverage used for relieving chills. Some of the Plains Indians boiled the edible bark of the Slippery Elm with buffalo meat to augment their diet in times of famine.

In modern herbal medicine, Slippery Elm bark is recommended as a nutritious food for convalescents and the elderly.

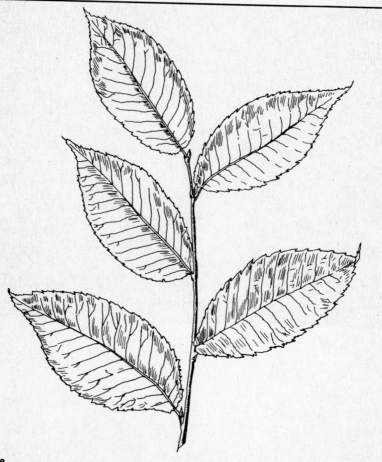

Smooth Sumac

Rhus glabra

This shrub grows in dry soil in most parts of Canada and the United States.

The Pawnee boiled the berries of the Smooth Sumac as a remedy for irregular menstruation and dysentery, and some tribes drank a cold infusion for fever and colds. The Creek had similar uses for the root. The Omaha boiled the root and drank the liquid for urinary disorders. They boiled the berries to make a wash to stop post-childbirth hemorrhage. The Creek mixed the roots and berries of Smooth Sumac in infusion with tobacco, and used the medicine thus obtained as a cure-all for chest complaints.

Other species of Sumac were in use among Indians, the specific species depending upon locale. The Comanche boiled the bark of *Rhus triloba*, Fragrant Sumac, and drank the liquid as a method of treating colds.

E. Barrie Kavasch

Spikenard

Aralia racemosa

Spikenard grows in the woods of eastern North America, from New Brunswick to Georgia, Minnesota and Missouri.

The Micmac of Eastern Canada made a salve of Spikenard berries mixed with lard or animal fat. This was used to treat wounds and cuts. The Ojibwa, Potawatomi, and Menominee made use of Spikenard roots for similar external applications. The Mohicans steeped Spikenard leaves in warm water and drank the liquid as a sedative for the respiratory system. The Cherokee drank a Spikenard-root tea to cure backache, a practice which was adopted by the settlers in the Great Smoky Mountains.

Spikenard has been employed in folk medicine to treat coughs and rheumatism and, externally, as a poultice for sores.

Flower cluster

Sunflower

Helianthus species

Many species of Sunflower grow in North America, most of them in the dry soils of the eastern region.

The Ojibwa employed the crushed root of the Sunflower as a poultice to draw blisters. The Hopi used parts of the Sunflower plant to treat insect bites, and an infusion of sunflower stems was reputed to be effective against malaria.

More often, however, the Sunflower was considered an important food item. The Iroquois and other tribes boiled the bruised, ripe seeds until the edible oil surfaced to be skimmed off for use as food. The Loretto Indians of Canada cooked the nutritious seeds in corn soup. Other tribes ate the seeds raw or roasted. Some tribes pounded the dried kernels into powder and made breads, cakes, and soups from the meal. A palatable coffee has been brewed with the roasted seeds.

E. Barrie Kavasch

Sweet Flag
or Calamus

Acorus calamus

This herb grows in damp or swampy areas from Nova Scotia to Ontario, Minnesota, Louisiana and Kansas.

Various Indian tribes used Calamus root as a remedy for colds, coughs, and stomach disorders. The root contains asarone, which is a hallucinogen. The Meskwaki Indians used the boiled root of Sweet Flag as a poultice for burns and scalds. Plains Indian tribes chewed the root of the plant as a remedy for toothache. Montana Indians boiled Sweet Flag root and drank the liquid in an effort to induce abortion. The Winnebago and the tribes of the Dakota federation made use of decoction of the root as a diaphoretic in fevers.

E. Barrie Kavasch

42

Wild Cherry
or Chokecherry

Prunus serotina

This large tree grows as far north as southern Ontario, as far south as Florida and Texas, and as far west as Dakota and Kansas.

The Chippewa amputated gangrenous frozen legs and arms and finished the operation with a poultice of pounded Wild Cherry bark applied to the stump. Some of the tribes boiled Wild Cherry twigs for a tonic beverage, and most of them regarded it as a blood purifier and as a treatment for tuberculosis. The Meskwaki brewed a sedative tea of the root-bark, a practice which was quickly adopted into the folk medicine of the white man.

The cherries were eaten raw or dried for the future. They were also used in soups and stews, and mixed with meat. Sometimes the cherries ended up as an ingredient in pemmican.

All parts of the Wild Cherry contain hydrocyanic acid. The bark has been included in the *United States Pharmacopoeia* since 1820, as a sedative and cough suppressant.

J.E. Underhill

E. Barrie Kavasch

Wild Ginger

Asarum canadense

A perennial herb, this plant is found in the woods from New Brunswick to Manitoba and south to North Carolina and Kansas.

The Canadian Montagnais used Wild Ginger root for a number of illnesses. The Meskwaki used the root in decoction for earache, throat problems, and stomach disorders. Several tribes of Canada and the United States considered the root a seasoning to make food more palatable and safe to eat. Two antibiotics have been discovered in the root.

The tribes also used Wild Ginger root to relieve palpitations of the heart, with the Catawba making use of a related species, *Asarum arifolium,* as a cardiac medication.

In official and folk medicine, Wild Ginger root has been employed as a stimulant, tonic and diaphoretic.

J.E. Underhill

Wild Lettuce

Lactuca virosa and other species

Wild Lettuce, from which is derived lactucarium (Lettuce Opium), is found in moist woods and clearings throughout most of North America. It was valued as a narcotic and sedative.

The Menominee and the Yokias of Mendocino County, California applied the milky juice of a freshly-picked Wild Lettuce plant as a remedy for the eruptions of poison ivy. Women of the Flambeau Ojibwa and Meskwaki tribes drank a tea of Wild Lettuce leaves to promote milk secretion following childbirth.

The settlers used the hardened juice of Wild Lettuce as a substitute for opium, giving the lactucarium the name "Lettuce Opium." It was used for sedation and as a narcotic in cases of pain.

E. Barrie Kavasch

E. Barrie Kavasch

Wintergreen

Gaultheria procumbens

Wintergreen was in widespread use among the Indians of North America. The Delawares of the northeastern United States and the Connecticut Mohicans made a tea of the leaves and drank the liquid as a remedy for kidney problems. The Canadian Montagnais administered Wintergreen tea to victims of paralysis. The Onondaga of the Iroquois Confederation ate the balsamic berries of Wintergreen as a medicine invigorating to the stomach. Various tribes made use of Wintergreen tea as a remedy for rheumatism, fevers, lumbago, asthma, and as a tonic.

The plant was adopted into early colonial medicine. Oil of Wintergreen has been listed in the *United States Pharmacopoeia* from 1820 until the present time.

Yellow Parilla
or Moonseed

TOXIC

Menispermum canadense

This perennial vine is found growing beside streams from western Quebec to Manitoba and south to Georgia and Arkansas.

The root is both diuretic and laxative, and the Pillager Ojibwa used it for these purposes. Records of other Indian usage of this plant are sketchy, doubtless because of the high toxicity of the root. This factor could certainly cause a certain amount of hesitation in usage.

In standard herbal medicine, the dried roots of Yellow Parilla have been used as a tonic and substitute for Sarsaparilla, *Smilax officinalis,* which contains the male hormone, testosterone. The dried rhizome of Yellow Parilla was listed in the *United States Pharmacopoeia* between 1882-1905 as a tonic and diuretic.

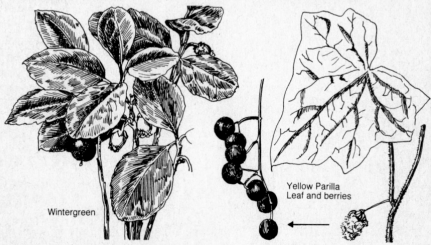

Yellow Parilla
Leaf and berries

Wintergreen

Further Reading

American Pharmaceutical Association. *United States National Formulary.* XIV - 14th edition. Washington: The Association, 1975.

BLACK, Marmalade. *It's the Berries.* Hancock House Publishers Ltd., 1977.

DENSMORE, Francis. *How The Indians Use Wild Plants For Food Medicine and Crafts.* N.Y: Dover Publications, 1974.

DOMICO, Terry. *Wild Harvest.* Hancock House Publishers Ltd., 1979.

FERNALD, Merritt L. *Gray's Manual of Botany,* 8th ED. N.Y: D. Van Nostrand Co., 1970.

GLEASON, Henry A. *Britton & Brown Illustrated Flora of Northeastern U.S. & Canada.* N.Y: the NYBG., 1952.

KAVASCH, E. Barrie. *Guide to Eastern Mushrooms.* Hancock House Publishers Ltd., 1981.

———————————. *Guide to Northeastern Wild Edibles.* Hancock House Publishers Ltd., 1981.

———————————. *Native Harvests: Botanicals & Recipes of the American Indians.* Random House, Inc., 1979.

MILLSPAUGH, Charles F. *American Medicinal Plants.* N.Y: Dover Publications, 1974.

SCULLY, Virginia. *A Treasury of American Indian Herbs.* N.Y: Dover Publications, 1970.

TANTAQUIDGEON, Gladys. *Folk Medicine of the Delaware & Related Algonkian Indians.* Harrisburg, PA: Pennsylvania Historical & Museum Comm., 1972.

UNDERHILL, J.E. *Northwestern Wild Berries.* Hancock House Publishers Ltd., 1980.

United States Pharmacopoeia. 19th revision (1975). Rockville, Maryland: United States Pharmacopeial Convention, Incorporated, 1975.

VOGEL, Virgil J. *American Indian Medicine.* Norman, Oklahoma: University of Oklahoma Press, 1970.

Index to Common & Latin Names